CW00693507

The Ultimate Beginners Plant Based Diet Recipe Book

The Ultimate Beginner's Guide to Tasty Plant-Based Diet Recipes to Stay Healthy, Lose Weight and Improve your Mood

Lisa Rice

Table of Contents

The information in the following pages is broadly considered a truthful and accurate account of facts and as such, any inattention, use, or misuse of the information in question by the reader will render any resulting actions solely under their purview. There are no scenarios in which the publisher or the original author of this work can be in any fashion deemed liable for any hardship or damages that may befall them after undertaking information described herein.

Additionally, the information in the following pages is intended only for informational purposes and should thus be thought of as universal. As befitting its nature, it is presented without assurance regarding its prolonged validity or interim quality. Trademarks that are mentioned are done without written consent and can in no way be considered an endorsement from the trademark holder.

Introduction

A plant-based diet is a diet based primarily on whole plant foods. It is identical to the regular diet we're used to already, except that it leaves out foods that are not exclusively from plants. Hence, a plant-based diet does away with all types of animal-sourced foods, hydrogenated oils, refined sugars, and processed foods. A whole food plant-based diet comprises not just fruits and vegetables; it also consists of unprocessed or barely-processed oils with healthy monounsaturated fats (like extra-virgin olive oil), whole grains, legumes (essentially lentils and beans), seeds and nuts, as well as herbs and spices.

What makes a plant-based meal (or any meal) fun is the manner with which you make them; the seasoning process; and the combination process that contributes to a fantastic flavor and makes every meal unique and enjoyable. There are lots of delicious recipes (all plant-centered), which will prove helpful in when you intend making mouthwatering, healthy plant-based dishes for personal or household consumption. Provided you're eating these plant-based foods regularly, you'll have very problems with fat or diseases that result from bad dietary habits, and there would be no need for excessive calorie tracking. Plant-based diet recipes are versatile; they range from colorful Salads to Lentil Stews, and Bean Burritos. The recipes also draw influences from around the globe, with Mexican, Chinese, European, Indian cuisines all part of the vast array of plant-based recipes available to choose from. Why You Ought to Reduce Your Intake of Processed and Animal-Based Foods. You have likely heard over and over that processed food has adverse effects on your health. You might have also been told repeatedly to stay away from foods with lots of preservatives;

nevertheless, nobody ever offered any genuine or concrete facts about why you ought to avoid these foods and why they are unsafe. Consequently, let us properly dissect it to help you properly comprehend why you ought to stay away from these healthy eating offenders. They have massive habit-forming characteristics. Humans have a predisposition towards being addicted to some specific foods; however, the reality is that the fault is not wholly ours. Every one of the unhealthy treats we relish now and then triggers the dopamine release in our brains. This creates a pleasurable effect in our brain, but the excitement is usually short-lived. The discharged dopamine additionally causes an attachment connection gradually, and this is the reason some people consistently go back to eat certain unhealthy foods even when they know it's unhealthy and unnecessary. You can get rid of this by taking out that inducement completely. They are sugar-laden and plenteous in glucose-fructose syrup. Animal-based and processed foods are laden with refined sugars and glucose-fructose syrup which has almost no beneficial food nutrient. An ever-increasing number of studies are affirming what several people presumed from the start; that genetically modified foods bring about inflammatory bowel disease, which consequently makes it increasingly difficult for the body to assimilate essential nutrients. The disadvantages that result from your body being unable to assimilate essential nutrients from consumed foods rightly cannot be overemphasized. Processed and animal-based food products contain plenteous amounts of refined carbohydrates. Indeed, your body requires carbohydrates to give it the needed energy to run body capacities. In any case, refining carbs dispenses with the fundamental supplements; in the way that refining entire grains disposes of the whole grain part. What remains, in the wake of refining, is what's considered as empty carbs or empty calories. These can negatively affect the metabolic system in your body by sharply increasing your blood sugar and insulin quantities. They contain lots of synthetic ingredients. At the point when your body is taking in non-natural ingredients, it regards them as foreign substances. Your body treats them as a health threat. Your body isn't accustomed to identifying synthetic compounds like sucralose or these synthesized sugars. Hence, in defense of your health against this foreign "aggressor," your body does what it's capable of to safeguard your health. It sets off an immune reaction to tackle this "enemy" compound, which indirectly weakens your body's general disease alertness, making you susceptible to illnesses. The concentration and energy expended by your body in ensuring your immune system remain safe could instead be devoted somewhere else. They contain constituent elements that set off an excitable reward sensation in your body. A part of processed and animal-based foods contain compounds like glucose-fructose syrup, monosodium glutamate, and specific food dyes that can trigger some addiction. They rouse your body to receive a benefit in return whenever you consume them. Monosodium glutamate, for example, is added to many store-bought baked foods. This additive slowly conditions your palates to relish the taste. It gets mental just by how your brain interrelates with your taste sensors.

This reward-centric arrangement makes you crave it increasingly, which ends up exposing you to the danger of over consuming calories.

For animal protein, usually, the expression "subpar" is used to allude to plant proteins since they generally have lower levels of essential amino acids as against animal-sourced protein. Nevertheless, what the vast majority don't know is that large amounts of essential amino acids can prove detrimental to your health. Let me break it down further for you.

Lentil Bean Salad

Preparation time: 10 Minutes

Cooking Time: 20 Minutes

Serving: 2

Ingredients:

- 15 ½ oz. Kidney Beans

- ¾ cup Red Lentils, dried

- 4 Spring Onions, sliced

- 1 Red Bell Pepper, sliced

- Salt & Pepper, to taste

- ½ cup Tomato Puree

Directions:

1. For making this easy salad, place red lentils and vegetable broth in a saucepan and heat it over medium-high heat.

2. After that, combine all the **Ingredients:** in a large mixing bowl and toss well.

3. To this, stir in the tomato puree and toss again.

4. Now, taste for seasoning and spoon in more salt and pepper.

5. Serve and enjoy.

Tip: If desired, you can spoon in lemon juice.

Nutrition:

Calories: 557Kcal

Proteins: 40g

Carbohydrates: 101g

Fat: 1.5g

Appetizers

Spiced Chickpeas

Preparation time: 5 minutes

Cooking time: 20 minutes

Servings: 4

Ingredients:

- 19 ounces cooked chickpeas

- 3/4 teaspoon salt

- 2 teaspoons tandoori spice blend

- 1 tablespoon olive oil

Directions:

1. Switch on the air fryer, insert the fryer basket, then shut it with the lid, set the frying temperature 390 degrees F, and let it preheat for 5 minutes.

2. Meanwhile, take a large bowl, place chickpeas in it, add remaining **Ingredients:** and toss until mixed.

3. Open the preheated fryer, place half of the chickpeas in it, close the lid and cook for 10 minutes until golden brown and cooked, shaking halfway.

4. When done, the air fryer will beep, then open the lid, transfer chickpeas to a dish and cover with foil to keep them warm.

5. Cook the remaining half of the chickpeas in the same manner and serve straight away.

Nutrition:

Calories: 140 Cal

Fat: 5 g

Carbs: 17 g

Protein: 6 g

Fiber: 4 g

Fried Ravioli

Preparation time: 5 minutes

Cooking time: 24 minutes

Servings: 4

Ingredients:

- 8 ounces frozen vegan ravioli, thawed

- 1 teaspoon garlic powder

- 1 teaspoon dried oregano

- 1/4 teaspoon ground black pepper

- 1/4 teaspoon salt

- 1 teaspoon dried basil

- 2 teaspoons nutritional yeast

- 1/2 cup panko bread crumbs

- 1/4 cup chickpeas liquid

- 1/2 cup marinara

- Olive oil spray

Directions:

1. Switch on the air fryer, insert the fryer basket, then shut it with the lid, set the frying temperature 390 degrees F, and let it preheat for 5 minutes.

2. Meanwhile, place bread crumbs in a shallow dish, add nutritional yeast and all the herbs and spices and stir until mixed.

3. Take a bowl, pour in chickpeas liquid in it, then dip ravioli in it and dredge into bread crumbs mixture until evenly coated.

4. Open the preheated fryer, place ravioli in it in a single layer, spray with olive oil, close the lid and cook for 12 minutes until golden brown and cooked, turning and spraying with oil halfway.

5. When done, the air fryer will beep, then open the lid, transfer ravioli to a dish and cover with foil to keep them warm.

6. Cook remaining ravioli in the same manner and then serve straight away.

Nutrition:

Calories: 150 Cal

Fat: 2 g

Carbs: 27 g

Protein: 5 g

Fiber: 2 g

Sweet Potato Tots

Preparation time: 5 minutes

Cooking time: 28 minutes

Servings: 25

Ingredients:

- 2 cups sweet potato puree

- 1/2 teaspoon ground cumin

- 1/2 teaspoon salt

- 1/2 teaspoon ground coriander

- 1/2 cup Panko breadcrumbs

- Olive oil spray

Directions:

- Switch on the air fryer, insert the fryer basket, then shut it with the lid, set the frying temperature 390 degrees F, and let it preheat for 5 minutes.

- Meanwhile, take a large bowl, place all the **Ingredients:** in it, stir until well combined, and then shape the mixture into twenty-five tots, each about 1 tablespoon.

- Open the preheated fryer, place sweet potato tots in it in a single layer, spray with olive oil, close the lid and cook for 14 minutes until golden brown and cooked, turning and spraying with oil halfway.

- When done, the air fryer will beep, then open the lid, transfer tots to a dish and cover with foil to keep them warm.

- Cook remaining tots in the same manner and then serve straight away.

Nutrition:

Calories: 26 Cal

Fat: 0.2 g

Carbs: 6 g

Protein: 0 g

Fiber: 2 g

Kale Chips

Preparation time: 5 minutes

Cooking time: 5 minutes

Servings: 2

Ingredients:

- 4 cups kale leaves, stems removed

- 1/4 teaspoon salt

- 2 teaspoons ranch seasoning, vegan

- 1 tablespoon nutritional yeast

- 2 tablespoons olive oil

Directions:

- Switch on the air fryer, insert the fryer basket, then shut it with the lid, set the frying temperature 370 degrees F, and let it preheat for 5 minutes.

- Meanwhile, take a medium bowl, add kale chips and remaining **Ingredients:** and toss until coated.

- Open the preheated fryer, place kale in it, close the lid and cook for 5 minutes until golden brown and cooked, shaking halfway.

- When done, the air fryer will beep and then open the lid and transfer kale chips to a dish.

- Serve straight away.

Nutrition:

Calories: 98 Cal

Fat: 4 g

Carbs: 15.7 g

Protein: 0 g

Fiber: 2.7 g

Avocado Fries

Preparation time: 5 minutes

Cooking time: 10 minutes

Servings: 4

Ingredients:

- 1 medium avocado, peeled, pitted, sliced

- 1/2 teaspoon salt

- 1/2 cup panko breadcrumbs

- 1/4 cup chickpeas liquid

- Olive oil spray

Directions:

- Switch on the air fryer, insert the fryer basket, then shut it with the lid, set the frying temperature 390 degrees F, and let it preheat for 5 minutes.

- Meanwhile, take a shallow bowl, place breadcrumbs in it, season with salt, and stir until combined.

- Take another shallow bowl, pour in chickpeas liquid, dip avocado slices in it and then dredge into breadcrumbs mixture until coated.

- Open the preheated fryer, place avocado slices in it in a single layer, spray with olive oil, close the lid and cook for 10 minutes until golden brown and cooked, shaking, and spraying with oil halfway.

- When done, the air fryer will beep and then open the lid and transfer avocado fries to a dish.

- Serve straight away.

Nutrition:

Calories: 132 Cal

Fat: 11.1 g

Carbs: 6.6 g

Protein: 4 g

Fiber: 4 g

Buffalo Cauliflower Wings

Preparation time: 10 minutes

Cooking time: 40 minutes

Servings: 4

Ingredients:

- 1 large head cauliflower, cut into florets

- 1 teaspoon minced garlic

- 1/2 cup Frank red hot sauce

- 2 tablespoons almond butter

- 1 cup of soy milk

- Olive oil spray

For the Batter:

- 1 cup almond flour

- 1/4 teaspoon dried chipotle chili

- 1/4 teaspoon cayenne pepper

- 1 teaspoon granules of chicken bouillon, vegan

- 1/4 teaspoon paprika

- 1/4 teaspoon red chili powder

Directions:

1. Switch on the air fryer, insert the fryer basket, then shut it with the lid, set the frying temperature 390 degrees F, and let it preheat for 5 minutes.

2. Meanwhile, prepare the batter and for this, take a large bowl, place all its **Ingredients:** in it and whisk until smooth batter comes together.

3. Then add cauliflower florets in it and toss until well coated.

4. Open the preheated fryer, place cauliflower florets in it in a single layer, close the lid and cook for 20 minutes until golden brown and cooked, turning and spraying with oil halfway.

5. Meanwhile, prepare the sauce and for this, take a small saucepan, place it over medium-high heat, add butter in it, stir in garlic and hot sauce, bring the mixture to boil and then simmer over medium heat until thickened, covering the pan.

6. When done, the air fryer will beep, then open the lid, transfer cauliflower florets to a large dish and cover with foil to keep them warm.

7. Cook remaining cauliflower florets, in the same manner, add them to the bowl, then pour prepared sauce over them and toss until well coated.

8. Serve straight away.

Nutrition:

Calories: 129 Cal

Fat: 1 g

Carbs: 24 g

Protein: 7 g

Fiber: 4 g

Baked Potatoes

Preparation time: 5 minutes

Cooking time: 40 minutes

Servings: 4

Ingredients:

- 4 large baking potatoes

- 4 tablespoons chopped parsley

- 1 teaspoon garlic powder

- 2 teaspoons ground black pepper

- 2 teaspoons salt

- 2 tablespoons olive oil

- 4 tablespoons almond butter, divided

Directions:

1. Switch on the air fryer, insert the fryer basket, then shut it with the lid, set the frying temperature 400 degrees F, and let it preheat for 5 minutes.

2. Meanwhile, brush potatoes with oil, then season with garlic powder, salt, and black pepper, and sprinkle with parsley.

3. Open the preheated fryer, place potatoes in it, close the lid and cook for 40 minutes until golden brown and cooked, turning and spraying with oil halfway.

4. When done, the air fryer will beep and then open the lid and transfer potatoes to a dish.

5. Open the potatoes by slicing them in half lengthwise, top each potato with 1 tablespoon of butter and serve.

Nutrition:

Calories: 161 Cal

Fat: 0.2 g

Carbs: 37 g

Protein: 4.3 g

Fiber: 3.8 g

Roasted Almonds

Preparation time: 5 minutes

Cooking time: 6 minutes

Servings: 8

Ingredients:

- 2 cups almonds

- 1 tablespoon garlic powder

- 1/4 teaspoon ground black pepper

- 1 teaspoon paprika

- 1 tablespoon soy sauce

Directions:

1. Switch on the air fryer, insert the fryer basket, then shut it with the lid, set the frying temperature 320 degrees F, and let it preheat for 5 minutes.

2. Meanwhile, take a large bowl, add almonds in it, then add remaining **Ingredients:** and toss until mixed.

3. Open the preheated fryer, place almonds in it, close the lid and cook for 6 minutes until golden brown and cooked, shaking halfway.

4. When done, the air fryer will beep and then open the lid and transfer almonds to a dish.

5. Serve straight away.

Nutrition:

Calories: 7.7 Cal

Fat: 0.7 g

Carbs: 0.3 g

Protein: 0.3 g

Fiber: 0.1 g

Snacks and Side Dishes

Glazed Carrots

Preparation Time: 15 minutes

Cooking Time: 8 minutes

Servings: 4

Ingredients:

- 1-pound baby carrots, peeled
- 1 tablespoon Maple syrup
- 1 tablespoon olive oil
- 1 teaspoon coriander, ground
- 1/2 teaspoon minced garlic
- 1 teaspoon turmeric powder
- 1 tablespoon apple cider vinegar
- 1 tablespoon sesame seeds
- 1/2 cup of water

Directions:

1. In a bowl, mix the carrots with the maple syrup and the other Ingredients, toss and leave aside for 10 minutes.

2. Transfer the mix in the instant pot. Add water and cook on Manual mode (High pressure) for 8 minutes.
3. Then make quick pressure release.
4. Transfer the mix in the serving bowls and serve.

Nutrition:

Calories: 172,

Fat: 4.9,

Fiber: 1.5,

Carbs: 6.1,

Protein: 4.3

Broccoli Puree

Preparation Time: 15 minutes

Cooking Time: 15 minutes

Servings: 6

Ingredients:

- 1 pound broccoli florets
- 1/3 cup almond milk
- 1 cup of water
- 1 teaspoon dried oregano
- 1/2 teaspoon coriander, ground

Directions:

1. Put the broccoli and the water in the instant pot and close the lid.
2. Cook on Manual mode (High pressure) for 15 minutes. Use natural pressure release for 10 minutes.
3. Strain, transfer to the food processor, add the rest of the Ingredients and pulse.
4. Divide between plates and serve.

Nutrition:

Calories: 182,

Fat: 3.8,

Fiber: 4.8,

Carbs: 11.1,

Protein: 2

Lemon Cauliflower

Preparation Time: 7 minutes

Cooking Time: 8 minutes

Servings: 4

Ingredients:

- 1 pound cauliflower florets
- 1 teaspoon lemon zest
- 1 tablespoon lemon juice
- 1 teaspoon turmeric powder
- 1 teaspoon black pepper
- 1 teaspoon Pink salt
- 1 tablespoon fresh dill, chopped
- 1/4 cup vegetable broth
- 1 tablespoon olive oil

Directions:

In the instant pot, mix the cauliflower with the lemon juice, zest and the other Ingredients, close the lid and cook on Manual mode for 8 minutes.

Allow natural pressure release.

Nutrition:

Calories: 205,Fat: 4.5, Fiber: 3.3, Carbs: 14.5, Protein: 4.2

Lemongrass Rice

Preparation Time: 15 minutes

Cooking Time: 15 minutes

Servings: .3

Ingredients:

- 1 cup wild rice
- 1 cup vegetable broth
- 1 tablespoon lemongrass, chopped
- 1 teaspoon turmeric powder
- 1 teaspoon oregano, dried
- 1 tablespoon almond butter
- 3/4 teaspoon ground nutmeg
- 1/3 teaspoon Pink salt

Directions:

Put quinoa in an instant pot.

Add the rest of the Ingredients and toss. Close the lid, seal it, and set Manual mode (high pressure).

Cook for 15 minutes and allow natural pressure release for 10 minutes.

Divide between plates and serve.

Nutrition:

Calories: 225,

Fat: 7.1,

Fiber: 4.6,

Carbs: 22.3,

Protein: 10.8

Chives Couscous

Preparation Time: 15 minutes

Cooking Time: 5 minutes

Servings: 4

Ingredients:

1 1/2 cup yellow couscous

2 cups of water

1 tablespoon chives, chopped

1 teaspoon cumin, ground

1 teaspoon coriander, ground

1 teaspoon cayenne pepper

1 tablespoon olive oil

1 teaspoon salt

Directions:

Preheat instant pot on Saute mode for 3 minutes.

Pour olive oil inside it and add couscous.

Stir it gently and saute for 2 minutes.

Add the rest of the Ingredients and toss. Close the
lid. Set manual mode (High pressure).

Cook the side dish for 2 minutes.

Release the pressure manually for 10 minutes.

Nutrition:

Calories: 96,

Fat: 3.6,

Fiber: 0.8,

Carbs: 11.5,

Protein: 4.5

Coconut Cauliflower Mix

Preparation Time: 10 minutes

Cooking Time: 10 minutes

Servings: 6

Ingredients:

- 1 pound cauliflower florets
- 1 cup of water
- 1/4 cup of coconut milk
- 1 tablespoon coconut yogurt
- 1 teaspoon salt
- 1 teaspoon hot paprika
- 1 teaspoon Italian seasoning
- 1 tablespoon chives, chopped

Directions:

Place cauliflower and water in the instant pot. Add salt and close the lid.

Cook the vegetables on Manual mode for 10 minutes.

Then use quick pressure release.

Open the lid, drain water and mash the cauliflower.

Add the rest of the Ingredients, stir well and serve.

Nutrition:

Calories: 211,

Fat: 4.6,

Fiber: 5.3,

Carbs: 24.2,

Protein: 3.9

Peppers Bowl

Preparation Time: 10 minutes

Cooking Time: 10 minutes

Servings: 2

Ingredients:

  1 pound red bell peppers, roughly sliced

  1/2 red onion, chopped

  1 teaspoon salt

  1 teaspoon black pepper

  1 teaspoon chili powder

  1/2 jalapeno pepper, chopped

  1/2 cup vegetable stock

  1/4 teaspoon ground coriander

  1 teaspoon dried rosemary

  1 teaspoon olive oil

Directions:

In the instant pot, mix the peppers with the onion, salt and the other Ingredients except the stock, set the pot on Saute mode and saute for 3 minutes.

Then the stock. Close the lid and set manual mode (High pressure) for 7 minutes.

Make a quick pressure release.

Transfer into the bowls.

Nutrition:

Calories: 201,

Fat: 4.3,

Fiber: 3.8,

Carbs: 14.3,

Protein: 5.3

Chili Cauliflower Rice

Preparation Time: 10 minutes

Cooking Time: 6 minutes

Servings: 4

Ingredients:

   2 1/2 cup cauliflower florets, grated

   1 teaspoon black pepper

   1 teaspoon oregano, dried

   1 teaspoon turmeric powder

   1 teaspoon salt

   1/2 cup of water

   1 teaspoon olive oil

   1 tablespoon chives, chopped

Directions:

In the instant pot, mix the cauliflower rice with black pepper and the other Ingredients and close the lid.

Set manual mode and cook on High for 6 minute. Make a quick pressure release.

Chill the cauliflower rice for 2-5 minutes before serving.

Nutrition:

Calories: 32,

Fat: 1.4,

Fiber: 1.6,

Carbs: 3.5,

Protein: 1.7

Potato Mash

Preparation Time: 10 minutes

Cooking Time: 9 minutes

Servings: 6

Ingredients:

- 1 and 1/2 pounds white potatoes, peeled, chopped
- 1 teaspoon salt
- 1/2 teaspoon hot paprika
- 1 teaspoon dill, dried
- 1 tablespoon coconut butter
- 1 teaspoon ground black pepper
- 1 cup vegetable broth
- 1 tablespoon fresh parsley, chopped

Directions:

Put potatoes, salt, and vegetable broth in the instant pot.

Close the lid and set manual mode. Cook on High for 9 minutes.

Then make quick pressure release, strain the sweet potatoes and mash until smooth.

Add the rest of the Ingredients, stir well and serve.

Nutrition:

Calories: 123,

Fat: 4.3,

Fiber: 2.2,

Carbs: 11.4,

Protein: 4.3

Red Cabbage and Carrots

Preparation Time: 10 minutes

Cooking Time: 7 minutes

Servings: 3

Ingredients:

1-pound red cabbage, shredded

2 carrots, peeled and grated

1 teaspoon turmeric powder

1 teaspoon coriander, ground

1 teaspoon black pepper

1 teaspoon salt

1/4 cup of coconut milk

3/4 cup almond milk

1/2 tablespoon chives, chopped

Directions:

In the instant pot, mix the cabbage with the carrots and the other Ingredients, toss and set manual mode (High pressure).

Cook the cabbage for 7 minutes. Then allow natural pressure release.

Transfer the meal into the serving bowls and cool down before serving.

Nutrition:

Calories: 182,

Fat: 5.1,

Fiber: 3.4,

Carbs: 12.3,

Protein: 2.6

Spaghetti Squash and Leeks

Preparation Time: 15 minutes

Cooking Time: 10 minutes

Servings: 4

Ingredients:

 2 leeks, sliced

 1 teaspoon chili powder

 1 teaspoon cumin, ground

 1 teaspoon onion powder

 1 teaspoon apple cider vinegar

 1-pound spaghetti squash, halved, seeds removed

 1 tablespoon Italian seasoning

1 cup water, for cooking

Directions:

Pour water in the instant pot and insert steamer rack.

Arrange spaghetti squash on the rack and close the lid.

Cook it on High for 10 minutes. Then allow natural pressure release for 5 minutes.

Check if the spaghetti squash is soft, shred the flesh with the help of a fork and transfer to a bowl.

Add the rest of the Ingredients, toss and serve.

Nutrition:

Calories: 110,

Fat: 1.7,

Fiber: 0,

Carbs: 4.3,

Protein: 0.8

Paprika Sweet Potato

Preparation Time: 10 minutes

Cooking Time: 11 minutes

Servings: 2

Ingredients:

- 2 sweet potatoes
- 2 teaspoons sweet paprika
- 1/2 teaspoon oregano, dried
- 1 teaspoon chili powder
- 1 teaspoon chives, chopped
- 1/2 cup of water

Directions:

Pour water in the instant pot and insert steamer rack.

Put potatoes on the rack and close the lid.

Set Manual mode (High pressure) and cook for 11 minutes. Then use quick pressure release.

Transfer the potatoes on the plate, cut into halves, sprinkle the rest of the Ingredients on top and serve.

Nutrition:

Calories: 159,

Fat: 3.4,

Fiber: 2.8,

Carbs: 33.8,

Protein: 3.6

Cinnamon Carrots

Preparation Time: 10 minutes

Cooking Time: 15 minutes

Servings: 4

Ingredients:

1 pound baby carrots, scrubbed

1/3 cup water

1 teaspoon ground cinnamon

1/4 teaspoon chili powder

1 teaspoon black pepper

Directions:

In the instant pot, mix the carrots with the water
and the other Ingredients, close the lid and
Manual mode (High pressure) for 15 minutes.
After this, use quick pressure release.
Divide between plates and serve.

Nutrition:

Calories: 147,

Fat: 0.5,

Fiber: 7.1,

Carbs: 9.9,

Protein: 4.3

Wild Rice and Corn

Preparation Time: 10 minutes

Cooking Time: 8 minutes

Servings: 4

Ingredients:

 1 cup wild rice

 1 tablespoon Italian seasoning

 1/4 cup corn kernels, canned

 1 teaspoon chili powder

 1 teaspoon salt

 2 cups vegetable broth

 1 tablespoon chives, chopped

 2 tablespoons olive oil

Directions:

Pour olive oil in the instant pot and set Saute mode.

Add rice and seasoning and cook for 2 minutes.

Add the rest of the Ingredients and toss.

Set Manual mode (High pressure) and close the lid. Seal it.

Cook rice for 6 minutes. Use quick pressure release.

Nutrition:

Calories: 254

Fat: 4.3

Fiber: 1.5

Carbs: 25.4

Protein: 5.4

Kale Polenta

Preparation Time: 5 minutes

Cooking Time: 8 minutes

Servings: 5

Ingredients:

 1 cup polenta

 1/2 cup kale, chopped

 1 teaspoon turmeric powder

 1 teaspoon smoked paprika

 4 cups vegetable broth

 2 tablespoons coconut milk

 1/2 teaspoon ground black pepper

 1 teaspoon salt

Directions:

Whisk together polenta and vegetable broth.

Pour mixture in the instant pot, add the rest of the
Ingredients and toss.

Close the lid and cook it on Manual mode (High
pressure) for 8 minutes. Use quick pressure
release/

Transfer cooked polenta in the bowl, stir and serve.

Nutrition:

Calories: 182,

Fat: 2.8,

Fiber: 1,

Carbs: 20.5,

Protein: 6.3

Black Bean Lime Dip

Preparation Time: 5 minutes

Cooking Time: 6 minutes

Servings: 4

Ingredients:

- 1.5 ounces cooked black beans
- 1 teaspoon minced garlic
- ½ of a lime, juiced
- 1 inch of ginger, grated
- 1/3 teaspoon salt
- 1/3 teaspoon ground black pepper
- 1 tablespoon olive oil

Directions:

1. Take a frying pan, add oil and when hot, add garlic and ginger and cook for 1 minute until fragrant.
2. Then add beans, splash with some water and fry for 3 minutes until hot.
3. Season beans with salt and black pepper, drizzle with lime juice, then remove the pan from heat and mash the beans until smooth pasta comes together.
4. Serve the dip with whole-grain breadsticks or vegetables.

Nutrition:

Calories: 374 Cal

Fat: 14 g

Carbs: 46 g

Protein: 15 g

Fiber: 17 g

Beetroot Hummus

Preparation Time: 10 minutes

Cooking Time: 60 minutes

Servings: 4

Ingredients:

- 15 ounces cooked chickpeas
- 3 small beets
- 1 teaspoon minced garlic
- 1/2 teaspoon smoked paprika
- 1 teaspoon of sea salt
- 1/4 teaspoon red chili flakes
- 2 tablespoons olive oil
- 1 lemon, juiced
- 2 tablespoon tahini
- 1 tablespoon chopped almonds
- 1 tablespoon chopped cilantro

Directions:

1. Drizzle oil over beets, season with salt, then wrap beets in a foil and bake for 60 minutes at 425 degrees F until tender.
2. When done, let beet cool for 10 minutes, then peel and dice them and place them in a food processor.

3. Add remaining ingredients and pulse for 2 minutes until smooth, tip the hummus in a bowl, drizzle with some more oil, and then serve straight away.

Nutrition:

Calories: 50.1 Cal

Fat: 2.5 g

Carbs: 5 g

Protein: 2 g

Fiber: 1 g

Basil Zucchinis And Eggplants

Preparation time: 10 minutes

Cooking time: 20 minutes

Servings: 4

Ingredients:

- 1 tablespoon olive oil
- 2 zucchinis, sliced
- 1 eggplant, roughly cubed
- 2 scallions, chopped
- 1 tablespoon sweet paprika
- Juice of 1 lime
- 1 teaspoon fennel seeds, crushed
- Salt and black pepper to the taste
- 1 tablespoon basil, chopped

Directions:

1. The scallions and fennel seeds need to be sautéed first in a pan since it is longer to cook.

2. The other ingredients will then be added, letting it simmer for 15 minutes.

Nutrition:

        Calories: 97

        Fat: 4

        Fiber: 2

        Carbohydrate: 6

        Protein: 2

Chard And Peppers Mix

Preparation time: 10 minutes

Cooking time: 20 minutes

Servings: 4

Ingredients:

- 2 tablespoons avocado oil
- 2 spring onions, chopped
- 2 tablespoons tomato passata
- 2 tablespoons capers, drained
- 2 green bell peppers, cut into strips
- 1 teaspoon turmeric powder
- A pinch of cayenne pepper
- Juice of 1 lime

- Salt and black pepper to the taste
- 1 bunch red chard, torn

Directions:

1. The spring onions, capers, turmeric and cayenne will be sautéed first in a pan since it is longer to cook.
2. The other ingredients will then be added, letting it simmer for 15 minutes.

Nutrition:

Calories 119

Fat: 7 g

Fiber: 3 g

Carbohydrate: 7 g

Protein 2 g

Balsamic Kale

Preparation time: 10 minutes

Cooking time: 20 minutes

Servings: 4

Ingredients:

- 1 tablespoon balsamic vinegar
- 2 tablespoons walnuts, chopped
- 1 lb. kale, torn
- 1 tablespoon olive oil
- 1 teaspoon cumin, ground
- 1 teaspoon chili powder
- 3 garlic cloves, minced
- 2 tablespoons cilantro, chopped

Directions:

1. The garlic and walnut needs to be sautéed first in a pan since they are longer to cook.
2. The other ingredients will then be added, toss and cook for 18 minutes.

Nutrition:

Calories: 170

Fat: 11 g

Fiber: 3 g

Carbohydrate: 7 g, Protein: 7 g

Cabbage And Green Beans

Preparation time: 10 minutes

Cooking time: 15 minutes

Servings: 4

Ingredients:

- 1 green cabbage head, shredded
- 2 cups green beans, trimmed and halved
- 2 tablespoons olive oil
- 1 teaspoon sweet paprika
- 1 teaspoon cumin, ground
- Salt and black pepper to the taste
- 1 tablespoon chives, chopped

Directions:

1. The cabbage and paprika needs to be sautéed first in a pan since they took longer to cook.
2. The other ingredients will then be added, letting it simmer for 13 minutes.

Nutrition:

Calories: 200

Fat: 4 g

Fiber: 2 g

Carbohydrate: 3 g

Protein: 7 g

Green Beans, Avocado And Scallions

Preparation time: 10 minutes

Cooking time: 20 minutes

Servings: 4

Ingredients:

- 1 lb. green beans, trimmed and halved
- 1 avocado, peeled, pitted and sliced
- 4 scallions, chopped
- 2 tablespoons olive oil
- 1 tablespoon lime juice
- Salt and black pepper to the taste
- A handful cilantro, chopped

Directions:

1. The scallions need to be sautéed first in a pan since it is longer to cook.
2. The other ingredients will then be added, toss and cook over medium heat for 18 minutes.

Nutrition:

Calories: 200

Fat: 5 g

Fiber: 2 g, Carbohydrate: 1 g, Protein: 3 g

Zucchini Hummus

Preparation Time: 5 minutes

Cooking Time: 0 minute

Servings: 8

Ingredients:

>   1 cup diced zucchini
>
>   1/2 teaspoon sea salt
>
>   1 teaspoon minced garlic
>
>   2 teaspoons ground cumin
>
>   3 tablespoons lemon juice
>
>   1/3 cup tahini

Directions:

>   Place all the ingredients in a food processor and pulse for 2 minutes until smooth.
>
>   Tip the hummus in a bowl, drizzle with oil and serve.

Nutrition:

>   Calories: 65 Cal
>
>   Fat: 5 g
>
>   Carbs: 3 g
>
>   Protein: 2 g
>
>   Fiber: 1 g

Chipotle and Lime Tortilla Chips

Preparation Time: 10 minutes

Cooking Time: 15 minutes

Servings: 4

Ingredients:

12 ounces whole-wheat tortillas

4 tablespoons chipotle seasoning

1 tablespoon olive oil

4 limes, juiced

Directions:

Whisk together oil and lime juice, brush it well on tortillas, then sprinkle with chipotle seasoning and bake for 15 minutes at 350 degrees F until crispy, turning halfway.

When done, let the tortilla cool for 10 minutes, then break it into chips and serve.

Nutrition:

Calories: 150 Cal

Fat: 7 g

Carbs: 18 g

Protein: 2 g

Fiber: 2 g

Carrot and Sweet Potato Fritters

Preparation Time: 10 minutes

Cooking Time: 8 minutes

Servings: 10

Ingredients:

> 1/3 cup quinoa flour
>
> 1½ cups shredded sweet potato
>
> 1 cup grated carrot
>
> 1/3 teaspoon ground black pepper
>
> 2/3 teaspoon salt
>
> 2 teaspoons curry powder
>
> 2 flax eggs

2 tablespoons coconut oil

Directions:

Place all the ingredients in a bowl, except for
oil, stir well until combined and then shape
the mixture into ten small patties

Take a large pan, place it over medium-high
heat, add oil and when it melts, add patties
in it and cook for 3 minutes per side until
browned.

Serve straight away

Nutrition:

Calories: 70 Cal

Fat: 3 g

Carbs: 8 g

Protein: 1 g

Fiber: 1 g

Buffalo Quinoa Bites

Preparation Time: 15 minutes

Cooking Time: 30 minutes

Servings: 20

Ingredients:

For the Bites:

> 1 cup cooked quinoa
>
> 15 ounces cooked white beans
>
> 3 tablespoons chickpea flour
>
> 1 medium shallot, peeled, chopped
>
> 3 cloves of garlic, peeled
>
> ½ teaspoon ground black pepper
>
> 1/2 teaspoon salt
>
> 1 teaspoon smoked paprika
>
> 1/4 cup vegan buffalo sauce

For the Dressing:

> 1/4 cup chives
>
> 2 tablespoons hemp hearts
>
> 1 tablespoon nutritional yeast
>
> 1 teaspoon garlic powder
>
> 1 teaspoon onion powder
>
> 1/2 teaspoon salt
>
> ½ teaspoon ground black pepper
>
> 2 teaspoons dried dill

1 lemon, juiced

1/4 cup tahini

3/4 cup water

Directions:

Prepare the bites, and for this, place half of the beans in a food processor, add garlic and shallots, and pulse for 2 minutes until mixture comes together.

Then add all the spices of the bites and buffalo sauce and pulse for 2 minutes until smooth. Add remaining beans along with chickpea flour and quinoa and pulse until just combined.

Tip the mixture in a dish, shape it in the dough, shape it into twenty balls, about the golf-ball size, and bake for 30 minutes at 350 degrees F until crispy and browned, turning halfway.

Meanwhile, prepare the dressing and for this, place all of its ingredients in a food processor and pulse for 2 minutes until smooth.

Serve bites with prepared dressing.

Nutrition:

Calories: 78 Cal

Fat: 3 g

Carbs: 9 g

Protein: 4 g

Fiber: 2 g

Tomato and Pesto Toast

Preparation Time: 5 minutes

Cooking Time: 0 minute

Servings: 4

Ingredients:

1 small tomato, sliced

¼ teaspoon ground black pepper

1 tablespoon vegan pesto

2 tablespoons hummus

1 slice of whole-grain bread, toasted

Hemp seeds as needed for garnishing

Directions:

Spread hummus on one side of the toast, top with tomato slices and then drizzle with pesto.

Sprinkle black pepper on the toast along with hemp seeds and then serve straight away.

Nutrition:

Calories: 214 Cal, Fat: 7.2 g, Carbs: 32 g Protein: 6.5 g, Fiber: 3 g

Avocado and Sprout Toast

Preparation Time: 5 minutes

Cooking Time: 0 minute

Servings: 4

Ingredients:

1/2 of a medium avocado, sliced

1 slice of whole-grain bread, toasted

2 tablespoons sprouts

2 tablespoons hummus

¼ teaspoon lemon zest

½ teaspoon hemp seeds

¼ teaspoon red pepper flakes

Directions:

Spread hummus on one side of the toast and then top with avocado slices and sprouts. Sprinkle with lemon zest, hemp seeds, and red pepper flakes and then serve straight away.

Nutrition:

Calories: 200 Cal, Fat: 10.5 g, Carbs: 22 g, Protein: 7 g, Fiber: 7 g

Apple and Honey Toast

Preparation Time: 5 minutes

Cooking Time: 0 minute

Servings: 4

Ingredients:

½ of a small apple, cored, sliced

1 slice of whole-grain bread, toasted

1 tablespoon honey

2 tablespoons hummus

1/8 teaspoon cinnamon

Directions:

Spread hummus on one side of the toast, top with apple slices and then drizzle with honey.

Sprinkle cinnamon on it and then serve straight away.

Nutrition:

Calories: 212 Cal

Fat: 7 g

Carbs: 35 g

Protein: 4 g

Fiber: 5.5 g

Thai Snack Mix

Preparation Time: 15 minutes

Cooking Time: 90 minutes

Servings: 4

Ingredients:

   5 cups mixed nuts

   1 cup chopped dried pineapple

   1 cup pumpkin seed

   1 teaspoon onion powder

   1 teaspoon garlic powder

   2 teaspoons paprika

1/2 teaspoon ground black pepper

1 teaspoon of sea salt

1/4 cup coconut sugar

1/2 teaspoon red chili powder

1 tablespoon red pepper flakes

1/2 tablespoon red curry powder

2 tablespoons soy sauce

2 tablespoons coconut oil

Directions:

Switch on the slow cooker, add all the ingredients in it except for dried pineapple and red pepper flakes, stir until combined and cook for 90 minutes at high heat setting, stirring every 30 minutes.

When done, spread the nut mixture on a baking sheet lined with parchment paper and let it cool.

Then spread dried pineapple on top, sprinkle with red pepper flakes and serve.

Nutrition:

Calories: 230 Cal

Fat: 17.5 g

Carbs: 11.5 g

Protein: 6.5 g, Fiber: 2 g

Zucchini Fritters

Preparation Time: 10 minutes

Cooking Time: 6 minutes

Servings: 12

Ingredients:

> 1/2 cup quinoa flour
>
> 3 1/2 cups shredded zucchini
>
> 1/2 cup chopped scallions
>
> 1/3 teaspoon ground black pepper
>
> 1 teaspoon salt
>
> 2 tablespoons coconut oil
>
> 2 flax eggs

Directions:

> Squeeze moisture from the zucchini by wrapping it in a cheesecloth and then transfer it to a bowl.
>
> Add remaining ingredients, except for oil, stir until combined and then shape the mixture into twelve patties.
>
> Take a skillet pan, place it over medium-high heat, add oil and when hot, add patties and cook for 3 minutes per side until brown.
>
> Serve the patties with favorite vegan sauce.

Nutrition:

       Calories: 37 Cal

       Fat: 1 g

       Carbs: 4 g

       Protein: 2 g

       Fiber: 1 g

Zucchini Chips

Preparation Time: 10 minutes

Cooking Time: 120 minutes

Servings: 4

Ingredients:

1 large zucchini, thinly sliced

1 teaspoon salt

2 tablespoons olive oil

Directions:

Pat dry zucchini slices and then spread them in an even layer on a baking sheet lined with parchment sheet.

Whisk together salt and oil, brush this mixture over zucchini slices on both sides and then bake for 2 hours or more until brown and crispy.

When done, let the chips cool for 10 minutes and then serve straight away.

Nutrition:

Calories: 54 Cal

Fat: 5 g

Carbs: 1 g, Protein: 0 g, Fiber: 0.3 g

Rosemary Beet Chips

Preparation Time: 10 minutes

Cooking Time: 20 minutes

Servings: 3

Ingredients:

    3 large beets, scrubbed, thinly sliced

    1/8 teaspoon ground black pepper

    ¼ teaspoon of sea salt

    3 sprigs of rosemary, leaves chopped

    4 tablespoons olive oil

Directions:

Spread beet slices in a single layer between two large baking sheets, brush the slices with oil, then season with spices and rosemary, toss until well coated, and bake for 20 minutes at 375 degrees F until crispy, turning halfway. When done, let the chips cool for 10 minutes and then serve.

Nutrition:

Calories: 79 Cal

Fat: 4.7 g

Carbs: 8.6 g

Protein: 1.5 g

Fiber: 2.5 g

Quinoa Broccoli Tots

Preparation Time: 10 minutes

Cooking Time: 20 minutes

Servings: 16

Ingredients:

> 2 tablespoons quinoa flour
>
> 2 cups steamed and chopped broccoli florets
>
> 1/2 cup nutritional yeast
>
> 1 teaspoon garlic powder
>
> 1 teaspoon miso paste
>
> 2 flax eggs
>
> 2 tablespoons hummus

Directions:

> Place all the ingredients in a bowl, stir until well combined, and then shape the mixture into sixteen small balls.
>
> Arrange the balls on a baking sheet lined with parchment paper, spray with foil and bake at 400 degrees F for 20 minutes until brown, turning halfway.
>
> When done, let the tots cool for 10 minutes and then serve straight away.

Nutrition:

Calories: 19 Cal

Fat: 0 g

Carbs: 2 g

Protein: 1 g

Fiber: 0.5 g

Spicy Roasted Chickpeas

Preparation Time: 10 minutes

Cooking Time: 20 minutes

Servings: 6

Ingredients:

30 ounces cooked chickpeas

½ teaspoon salt

2 teaspoons mustard powder

½ teaspoon cayenne pepper

2 tablespoons olive oil

Directions:

Place all the ingredients in a bowl and stir until well coated and then spread the chickpeas in an even layer on a baking sheet greased with oil.

Bake the chickpeas for 20 minutes at 400 degrees F until golden brown and crispy and then serve straight away.

Nutrition:

Calories: 187.1 Cal, Fat: 7.4 g,Carbs: 24.2 g, Protein: 7.3 g, Fiber: 6.3 g

Mango & Papaya After-Chop

Preparation time: 25 minutes

Cooking time: 0 minutes

Servings: 4

Ingredients:

1/4 of papaya, chopped

1 mango, chopped

1 Tablespoon coconut milk

1/2 teaspoon maple syrup

1 Tablespoon peanuts, chopped

Directions:

Cut open the papaya. Scoop out the seeds, chop.

Peel the mango. Slice the fruit from the pit, chop.

Put the fruit in a bowl. Add remaining

Ingredients:. Stir to coat.

Nutrition:

Calories 100,

Fats 1 g,

Carbohydrates 25 g,

Proteins 1 g

Sautéed Bosc Pears with Walnuts

Preparation time: 15 minutes

Cooking time: 16 minutes

Servings: 6

Ingredients:

2 Tablespoon salted butter

1/4 teaspoon cinnamon

1/4 teaspoon nutmeg, ground

6 Bosc pears, peeled, quartered

1 Tablespoon lemon juice

1/2 cup walnuts, chopped, toasted

Directions:

Melt butter in a skillet, add spices and cook for 30 seconds.

Add pears and cook for 15 minutes. Stir in lemon juice.

Serve topped with walnuts.

Nutrition:

Calories 220,

Fats 10 g,

Carbohydrates 31 g,

Proteins 2 g

Brown Rice Pudding

Preparation time: 5 minutes

Cooking time: 1 hour

Servings: 6

Ingredients:

    2 cups brown rice, cooked

    3 cups light coconut milk

    3 eggs

    1 cup brown sugar

    1 teaspoon vanilla

    1/2 teaspoon salt

    1/2 teaspoon cinnamon

    1/4 teaspoon nutmeg

Directions:

    Blend all **Ingredients:** well. Put mixture in a 2-
        quart casserole dish.

    Bake at 300 degree F for 90 minutes.

    Serve.

Nutrition:

Calories 330,

Fats 10 g,

Carbohydrates 52 g,

Proteins 5 g

Plant-based Taco Salad

Preparation time: 7 minutes

Cooking time: 30 minutes

Servings: 4

Ingredients:

- 1 15-ounce can chickpeas, rinsed, drained and dried well in a paper towel
- 2 teaspoon cumin, divided
- 2 teaspoons chili powder, divided
- 1/2 teaspoon sea salt, divided
- 1/4 teaspoon ground cinnamon
- 1 15-ounce can black beans, rinsed and drained
- 1/2 teaspoon garlic powder
- 1/2 teaspoon paprika
- 1/2 teaspoon cayenne
- 1/4 cup water
- 1 head Romaine lettuce, chopped
- 1 red bell pepper, diced
- 1 tomato, chopped
- 1 cup frozen corn kernels, thawed, drained and patted dried
- 1 avocado, diced
- Creamy Ranch Dressing

Directions:

Preheat the oven to 400 degrees, Fahrenheit and prepare a lipped baking sheet by covering the surface with parchment paper.

In a bowl, sprinkle the drained chickpeas with one teaspoon of the cumin, one teaspoon of the chili powder, a quarter teaspoon of the sea salt and the cinnamon. Toss to coat.

Pour this mixture onto the prepared baking sheet, spreading the chickpeas in a single layer. Bake for 10 minutes.

Shake the pan to turn over the chickpeas and bake for another 10 minutes. Remove from the oven and let cool.

Toss the black beans with the remaining garlic powder and salt, the paprika and the cayenne pepper; pour into a skillet over medium heat.

Add the water and stir, cooking for five to six minutes, until warmed through. Set the pan aside.

In a large bowl, toss the lettuce, bell pepper, tomatoes, corn and avocado.

Place the lettuce in four separate bowls. Spoon
the warm black bean mixture on top and
sprinkle with the chickpeas.

Drizzle on top as much dressing as you please
and stir it in.

Nutrition:

Calories 322,

Fats 7 g,

Carbohydrates 30 g,

Proteins 21 g

Raw Energy Squares

Preparation time: 30 minutes

Cooking time: 0 minutes

Servings: 6

Ingredients:

  2 cups Medjool dates, chopped and pitted

  2 cups cashews

  1/2 cup almonds

  3/4 cup powder, cocoa

  Sea salt, to taste

  2 Tablespoon vanilla extract

  3 Tablespoon cold water

Directions:

  Blend first five **Ingredients:** in a food
    processor.

  Add the vanilla and water, give a quick pulse.

  Put the dough into a pan, making an even
    layer.

  Cut into squares and serve.

Nutrition:

Calories 330,

Fats 10 g,

Carbohydrates 52 g, Proteins 5 g

Spiced Pecans

Preparation time: 15 minutes

Cooking time: 15 minutes

Servings: 12

Ingredients:

2 Tablespoon brown sugar

1/2 teaspoon sweet paprika

1/2 teaspoon chili powder

1/2 cup vegan butter, melted

4 cups pecans

Directions:

Preheat oven to 350 degree F.

Blend first five **Ingredients:**.

Pour in the butter and mix. Add the nuts and
toss to coat.

Spread the seasoned nuts on a baking sheet.
Roast for 15 minutes.

Nutrition:

Calories 232,

Fats 24 g,

Carbohydrates 6 g,

Proteins 2 g

Conclusion

In a nutshell, this cookbook offers you a world full of options to diversify your plant-based menu. People on this diet are usually seen struggling to choose between healthy food and flavor but, soon, they run out of the options. The selection of 250 recipes in this book is enough to adorn your dinner table with flavorsome, plant-based meals every day. Give each recipe a good read and try them out in the kitchen. You will experience tempting aromas and binding flavors every day.

The book is conceptualized with the idea of offering you a comprehensive view of a plant-based diet and how it can benefit the body. You may find the shift sudden, especially if you are a die-hard fan of non-vegetarian items. But you need not give up anything that you love. Eat everything in moderation.

The next step is to start experimenting with the different recipes in this book and see which ones are your favorites. Everyone has their favorite food, and you will surely find several of yours in this book. Start with breakfast and work your way through. You will be pleasantly surprised at how tasty a vegan meal really can be.

You will love reading this book, as it helps you to understand how revolutionary a plant-based diet can be. It will help you to make informed decisions as you move toward greater change for the greater good. What are you waiting for? Have you begun your journey on the path of the plant-based diet yet? If you haven't, do it now!

Now you have everything you need to get started making budget-friendly, healthy plant-based recipes. Just follow your basic shopping list and follow your meal plan to get started! It's easy to switch over to a plant-based diet if you have your meals planned out and temptation locked away. Don't forget to clean out your kitchen before starting, and you're sure to meet all your diet and health goals.

You need to plan if you are thinking about dieting. First, you can start slowly by just eating one meal a day, which is vegetarian and gradually increasing your number of vegetarian meals. Whenever you are struggling, ask your friend or family member to support you and keep you motivated. One important thing is also to be regularly accountable for not following the diet.

If dieting seems very important to you and you need to do it right, then it is recommended that you visit a professional such as a nutritionist or dietitian to discuss your dieting plan and optimizing it for the better.

No matter how much you want to lose weight, it is not advised that you decrease your calorie intake to an unhealthy level. Losing weight does not mean that you stop eating. It is done by carefully planning meals.

A plant-based diet is very easy once you get into it. At first, you will start to face a lot of difficulties, but if you start slowly, then you can face all the barriers and achieve your goal.

Swap out one unhealthy food item each week that you know is not helping you and put in its place one of the plant-based ingredients that you like. Then have some fun creating the many different recipes in this book. Find out what recipes you like the most so you can make them often and most of all; have some fun exploring all your recipe options.

Wish you good luck with the plant-based diet!

CPSIA information can be obtained
at www.ICGtesting.com
Printed in the USA
BVHW041741120421
604749BV00014B/432

9 781801 834582